William Henry Harrison Murray

Deacons

Out Door Orthodoxy

William Henry Harrison Murray

Deacons

Out Door Orthodoxy

ISBN/EAN: 9783743382589

Manufactured in Europe, USA, Canada, Australia, Japa

Cover: Foto ©Lupo / pixelio.de

Manufactured and distributed by brebook publishing software (www.brebook.com)

William Henry Harrison Murray

Deacons

DEACONS.

W. H. H. MURRAY,

AUTHOR OF "ADVENTURES IN THE WILDERNESS,"
"MUSIC-HALL SERMONS," &c., &c.

BOSTON:
HENRY L. SHEPARD AND COMPANY,
(LATE SHEPARD & GILL.)
1875.

Entered according to Act of Congress, in the year 1874, by
HENRY L. SHEPARD & CO.,
In the Office of the Librarian of Congress, at Washington.

STEREOTYPED BY C. J. PETERS & SON,
73 FEDERAL ST., BOSTON.

PRESS OF RAND, AVERY, & CO.

LIST OF ILLUSTRATIONS.

	PAGE.
Deacon Goodheart.	Frontispiece.
Out-door Orthodoxy, Head-piece	10
"Pretty soon the Sparks will begin to fly"	12
Deacon Slowup	19
"His Little Shrunken Cheeks actually puffed out"	21
"Bill Stevens assured his Wondering Followers".	23
"The Progressives were Jubilant . . . not so with the Conservatives"	24
"At this Point Deacon Slowup got the Floor"	28
"The Symbol of Christianity was a Rent Banner".	35
"It made the Sewing-Society lively for Two Weeks"	40
Deacon Sharpface.	43
"He listened to Every Sermon"	46
"His Wife knew that best"	47
"My Eyes are Open, Brother"	52
"These Cathedrals of Exclusiveness".	60
"It was Night"	67
"He twisted Himself about"	71
"The more he slid, the Louder he laughed"	74
"It was the Home of Desolation".	77
"He broke out, and sobbed Aloud," Tail-piece.	82

AUTHOR'S PREFACE.

ON giving "Deacons" to my publishers, and through them to the public, a word from the author may be expected, at least permitted.

The lecture was written to call the attention of the Church and people to the perversion and abuse of an office in our Congregational churches which was created to assist the pastors by relieving them from much of the detail work of the parish, that they might give their thoughts more entirely to the preaching of the Word; but which, through certain causes, to-day fulfils no such service.

In the second place, and above all, I wished to inculcate the sweet lesson of charity and forgiveness, both as regards practical alms-giving, and also as regards intellectual differences in matters of belief. With such a motive, the lecture was composed, and delivered first in Music Hall, 1871. When delivered first, there were only seventeen engagements secured for it; and, for reasons which I could never understand, nearly all the religious press were, directly or indirectly, unfriendly in their criticism of it. But there seemed to be something in it that the people were willing to hear; for it was called for over one hundred times that season, and has since been demanded by lyceums until it has been heard before almost every course in New England, and, I presume, by two hundred and fifty thousand people. It is to that portion of this large number, who, having heard the lecture, expressed the earnest wish that I would ultimately allow it to be published, that I now dedicate it. With me it has always been a favorite. Its composition gave me delight, and needed discipline; while by it I have been brought into pleasant relations with many delightful people, and have done something, I trust, to bring men into relations of kindness and brotherhood. That it may continue and perpetuate this influence, is the sincere wish of the author.

W. H. H. MURRAY.

✠ DEACONS ✠

– OUT DOOR ORTHODOXY –

In New England, ladies and gentlemen, the student of human nature runs across all sorts of characters. Classes and types are as distinct as geologic strata. The strictest individuality abounds everywhere. Now, a Frenchman is a Frenchman, an Englishman is an Englishman, and a Jew, as you all know, is a Jew, the world over. They represent their several nations. They are only the pattern of millions of others just like themselves. But here in New England it is different. Here there is no national type. A Yankee is a nation in himself. No one is like his neighbor. You cannot go into any New-England village, and find two men who look alike. You can scarcely go into a New-England family, and find two children who look alike. The blonde and the brunette, the light and dark haired, the lean and the stout, eat at the same family table, and bear the same family name. Bigotry and liberality sit side by side in the same church-pew. Progression and old-fogyism sing piously from the same hymn-book. New-England character is diversified. Like the scenery of the Adirondacks, every look you take at it is a revelation.

In nothing is this diversity, this antagonism of character, so prominent as in *ecclesiastical* affairs. When the descendant of the Puritan enters the realm of religion, his intense personality begins to stand forth. It is such a revelation of his inner nature as the tree makes of its nature, when, in June, it puts forth its leaves. In religious matters, the typical Yankee never shams. Cool, calculating, stoical, as to every thing else, touch him with a catechism, and you will see the flash of his eyes through the holes in his mask. Cautious and secretive in every thing else, he is frankness itself touching what he believes or does not believe, in reference to religion. You take a dozen men out of this audience to-night, and ask them what they think about total depravity, and you will find that each has a very positive opinion of his own. Assertion will be set over against assertion. Like knives drawn against each other, they will warm up as they proceed. Their language will sharpen until it cuts. By and by their tempers will clash. Pretty soon the sparks will begin to fly; and, before they have been at it half an hour, the doctrine will be proved by their conduct.

In respect to religion, then, the typical American is both individual and talkative. He cannot agree, and he cannot keep silent. He is a natural partisan. To argue, dispute, deny, is, with him, a matter of conscience. Every man here to-night is his own pope, and every man cordially believes that his pope is infallible.

From this diversity of views, this individuality and antagonism of opinion, sects arise, and denominations are multiplied in our midst. The American is not lacking in reverence for the Deity; that is not it: but he is determined to have a Deity that suits himself. In England, in France, in Germany, people are content to worship in one place. They accept one form of eccle-

"PRETTY SOON THE SPARKS WILL BEGIN TO FLY."

siastical government: they subscribe to one order of service. If they have differences, they are politely and decorously waived. The established order is recognized as essential, and tolerated if it is not admired. Progress is less rapid; but there is more peace and quietness than we have here. But with us the condition of things is entirely different. Independence of views is universal. The love of argument and the habit of disputation are national characteristics.

This is also noticeable in our history. New England was never harmonious within itself. In its principles, as well as in its administration of government, it existed the very embodiment of contradictions. Politically it was dedicated to freedom, and yet it held slaves. Its birth-cry was liberty of conscience; and yet it banished the peaceful Quaker, and scourged the Baptist through the streets of Boston. In name, in the voice of its own affirmation, it was a democracy; and yet, in point of fact, I presume, that, in no other country on the globe, were the lines between the poor and the rich, the titled and the unhonored, ever more sharply drawn. The parson of a New-England church, a century ago, was a great village dignitary, made such by no wish or effort of his own, but by the custom and habits of the age. He, with the "colonel" and "esquire" of the village, were the ruling potentates. These three men dictated its political, social, and religious life, to an extent that we, of freer habits of thought and speech, cannot realize. Their word was literally law. Nothing in the parish was undertaken without their co-operation. Nothing could prosper, that they and their families did not inaugurate, or at least favor.

This aristocratic element, strange to say, was most visible where we might expect it to be entirely absent, — in the administration of religion, — the religion, too, of the simple, unformal Saviour. The house of God, in which all mere human distinctions should fade away, was made to perpetuate these; and the sanctuary, even in the allotment of its sittings, became a sort of advertising card by which was proclaimed the social status of the worshippers. To be an officer of a church, in those days, was to be a dignitary. Office gave rank. It lifted the man himself, and lifted his family socially. What, in the scriptural appointment, designated a man for an humble service, in the New-England church elected him to a distinction, and ministered to his pride. Men naturally grew to love the honor, and forget the humility, of the original service, as founded in Stephen's time, until the office at last was given as a reward for uncommon piety, or what was supposed to be such; and the "deacon," instead of being a co-laborer with the pastor, releasing him from the detail work of the administration, came, at length, to be a kind of ornamental assistant at one of the two sacraments. The original service being lost sight of, the office came to be regarded as bestowing a certain rank and dignity upon the holder of it, which the appointing power itself could not justly take from him.

This anomalous state of things no longer exists. Politically, the democratic element has triumphed in our polity, until it has swept away the stately habits, and titles of address, that once marked distinctions in New England. If any of these gentlemen present should have occasion to address a letter to Patrick Finnegan or Michael O'Flaherty, they would, I presume, put the once honorable title of "Esquire" after the name; especially if they expected to be nominated to an office in their ward. The dominie is no longer a dignitary. I travel a good deal in the country, where I always make it a point to carry myself most ministerially. Indeed, I might say that I am noted in this respect. But I never see a row of little sunburnt, chubby-faced urchins ranged up against the side of the schoolhouse, hat in hand, as I move slowly, and with august expression on my features, past the little fellows, as I might have seen, had I filled the office which I hold a century ago.

But, although the "esquire" and "parson" have passed away, the "deacon" still lives; not as a class, but here and there as a remnant, an exception, we will say. Almost every church has one or more who represent the reverse of progress, of fitness for the office, of humility, of charity. Wherever you find one of this kind, he is a marked man. I can sit in the pulpit, and pick him out from among a thousand. He is as different from the mass of Christians, as a crab is from fish, or a zebra from cattle. I will run cursorily over the list. There is the bigoted, narrow-minded deacon. I knew one once so narrow-minded, that you had to hold him up, and look at him sidewise, to see that he had any mind at all. There, too, is the querulous deacon, who fights his pastor with the same fervor with which he prays for the heathen, and with about the same effect; and the heresy-hunting deacon, who watches the pulpit as a terrier does a rat-hole, in order to pounce upon some unfortunate sentence or quotation, and goes trotting down the centre-aisle after the benediction, his eyes fairly snapping with suppressed satisfaction that he has scented out one more proof that his pastor is "unsound in the faith." Then, there is the timid deacon: you all know him, afraid of the smallest thing, even his own shadow, and who is always worrying in his goodness, and trembling that his minister will do something to hurt his influence; forgetful of the great fact, which hangs like a pillar of cloud and fire before the path of every public man in America, that if he does what seems to him needed, and keeps in the main right, God will take care of his influence. And then, there is the old-fogy deacon, — the best specimen I ever saw was nominally only forty-three years of age, though in point of fact he was older than Methuselah; and the deacon who leads the choir, and knows better than the pastor how to select the hymns. And last, but not least, the deacon who studied two terms in the theological seminary, and whom the sewing-society of his native village was educating to send as a missionary to the heathen, but who didn't go, for two reasons: first, because the sewing-society got into a sisterly fight, and broke up, and the funds failed; and, second, because he himself failed to pass his examination at the end of the second term; all of which was ordered by Providence in mercy to the heathen. These are several of the typical deacons which I have met and known in my service and journeying up and down through New England. Descending now from the general to the specific, friends, I will sketch you the portrait of three in detail. The first I present to you is Deacon Slowup, senior deacon of the First Congregational Church of Fossilville. And I select an interesting and critical time in the history of this church, in order to get a suitable frame for the picture I am to paint.

A momentous event impended over Fossilville. The Congregational Church, of which Deacon Slowup was senior deacon, after much deliberation had voted, seventeen to four, to have a picnic. To be sure, this decision had not been reached without the expenditure of much time, and not a little manœuvring, on the part of those who had the matter in hand. It had taken three sewing-bees, four sociables, two sermons, thirty-nine pastoral visitations, and one church-meeting, to accomplish it.

DEACON SLOWUP.

But the pastor and his coadjutors had carried the day, and the thing was settled. As I have said, it was a momentous event; and, as the appointed day drew near, Fossilville was convulsed as never before. The children

"HIS LITTLE SHRUNKEN CHEEKS ACTUALLY PUFFED OUT."

were hilarious. They had never had a picnic; and hence their knowledge was beautifully indefinite. Tom Hazard said that it was a kind of Fourth of July without the fire-crackers. Little Jimmy Finch, — whose father was dead, and whose mother took in washing for a living, and had a pretty hard time of it in trying to clothe and feed the three little Finches, — Jimmy wished to know if it wouldn't be a kind of Thanksgiving; and when Martha Simpson assured him that it would be, only a great deal better, and told him that there would be puddings as big as he could lift, and bushel-baskets full of sandwiches, his little shrunken cheeks actually puffed out, and he loosened two buttons of his waistcoat in anticipation. Bill Stevens, a kind of oracle to the school, whose father was a doctor, and something of a wag, — Bill Stevens assured his wondering followers that it was a religious April Fool's Day, in which the deacons tripped each other up, the minister had a foot-race with the sexton, and old Miss Delia Mitchel would roll the trencher for four hours and a half with Col. Joshua Stubbs. He said he guessed he knew, for his father had told him so that very morning at breakfast.

But, if the little folks were excited, the elderly people were not less so.

The progressives were jubilant. They congratulated each other slyly on the streets, they squeezed the pastor's hand when they met him, they exchanged significant looks as they went into church of Sundays. They realized the magnitude of their triumph, and enjoyed it hugely. They felt that a brighter day was dawning for Fossilville. Not so with the conservatives. They

"BILL STEVENS ASSURED HIS WONDERING FOLLOWERS."

were in a state of solemn anxiety. They shook their heads gravely one at another as they went out of the meeting after the vote to hold the picnic was carried. When approached in conversation by the pastor, who wished to smooth their somewhat ruffled tempers, they said, "It was a momentous step, and a terrible responsibility for a church to take upon itself; but they hoped the Lord would overrule it for good." But they had

"THE PROGRESSIVES WERE JUBILANT. . . . NOT SO WITH THE CONSERVATIVES."

their fears; yes, they had their fears. Several of the more venerable female members, unable to endure the strain upon their nervous systems, took sick; and Dr. Stevens, for once, had his hands full. The morning before the picnic he sent an extra five-dollar bill to the financial committee, in a note in which he said that the enclosed was a business investment to encourage future picnics.

At last the evening preceding the day of the picnic came. A meeting for "all interested" had been called to meet at seven o'clock in the conference-room. I need not say that it was crowded. Everybody was there. The pastor called the meeting to order promptly, and invited Deacon Slowup to open with prayer. Now, the deacon had but one. It had served him well, on all occasions, for thirty-five years; but a dim suspicion flashed through his mind, as he arose, that it would not answer for a picnic. Everybody was on tiptoe of curiosity to see how he would begin. The deacon realized the gravity of the moment, and what there was at stake. He did his best to begin appropriately. It was too much. The tyranny of habit was too strong upon him. He hesitated, stammered, coughed, cleared his throat in the traditional way, and then gave it up. He swung into his old form, with a long breath of relief, and went through the whole thing, with all its verbal inflections, its vocal lapses and swellings, and snapped off the "Amen" with a little more than his customary vigor at the close.

He sat down. His prayer had manifestly affected not a few of his audience. Several handkerchiefs were visible. Flushed faces were everywhere. The pastor's eyes were moist. But he was a man of excellent nerve, and he controlled his voice; and the meeting proceeded to business. Several committees were called, and reported. At last they came to the committee on "Provisions." At this point the meeting reached its crisis. An unexpected event occurred.

A difference had arisen in the committee in respect to the sandwiches. It was not as to whether they should have sandwiches: that had been carried unanimously; but whether they should have *ham*-sandwiches, or *beef*-sandwiches. Upon this point the committee had been unable to agree; and "therefore," as the chairman repeated, "they had voted to refer the whole question to the church;" which they now did, and asked for instructions.

A moment of deathlike stillness followed this announcement. Everybody felt that they were on the eve of a terrible explosion. The pastor settled his face to a dead calm, and waited the development. At last a brother who was seated in the farthest corner of the room slowly arose, and said deliberately, " Mr. Chairman, in order to test the sense of the church, I move you, sir, that the committee be instructed to procure BEEF-sandwiches." The speaker had barely recovered his seat before another brother, on the opposite side of the room, was on his feet. " Mr. Chairman," said he, " I move to amend Bro. Go-ahead's motion by striking out the word 'beef,' and substituting the word 'ham,' before 'sandwiches.'" The ball was now opened, and at it they went. Fossilville was not lacking in local orators, and they were not inclined to let this opportunity slip. First the motion, then the amendment, was advocated; arguments from prophecy, and arguments from revelation, were adduced *pro* and *con*. History was cited, science appealed to, chemistry quoted. Beef was pronounced cheaper, ham the more scriptural. Motion was added to motion, amendment piled upon amendment. Ten o'clock came and no vote had been reached.

At this point Deacon Slowup got the floor. It was evident to all that he was powerfully wrought upon. He took the gravity of the occasion all in. To see this night he had been spared; for this emergency had

Providence caused him to be elected deacon. He arose to make the speech of his life.

"Brethren and sisters," he said, "this is indeed an eventful moment. If ever a people needed wisdom,

"AT THIS POINT DEACON SLOWUP GOT THE FLOOR."

we do at this time. It will be forty-three years next December since I was elected deacon of this church. I have seen many dark days in its history, but never such a season as this. I tremble for our future. Never did I expect to live to see the day when such a motion as this could be discussed in this church. Such a motion could never have been introduced when Dr. Longtongue, of sainted memory, occupied the pulpit in the room over our heads. Can any brother or sister who ever heard him preach suppose that he would have countenanced BEEF-sandwiches? Never. He would have died first. One brother says that he does not see what difference it makes. As an officer of the church, as a standard-bearer in this branch of Zion, I warn the brother against backsliding: he stands on slippery places. This church can not and will not tolerate Arminianism. Only last week I saw in 'The Phillipstown Gazette' an account of a picnic that the Unitarian Church in Heresyborough was to hold; and it went on to say that they had voted to have six thousand five hundred beef-sandwiches. My friends, who can estimate the influence of those six thousand five hundred beef-sandwiches? It is by such subtle and cunning methods that error is being promulgated in the land. And now let me ask, Are our children to be filled to-morrow with Unitarianism, and the church make no protest? From the day when it was founded, the First

Congregational Church of Fossilville has always believed in ham-sandwiches. Not that we ever really had them; but that was our faith, we believed in them. I do to-night. I wish every child in the land had a ham-sandwich. I was brought up on ham: it was instilled into me in my youth. I love it to-night, and always shall. 'Ham' is a scriptural word. I do not at this minute recall the passage; but it can be found in the Bible. 'Beef' is a secular word: it is carnal. It has been appropriated by error. Remember, you are establishing a precedent. If we have beef this year, we shall have beef next year, our children will grow to love it, and we shall never have any thing but beef."

The deacon sank into his seat overpowered with emotion caused by the picture he had drawn. Not a word more was said. The pastor, a young man, dismissed the meeting without a syllable, and resigned his charge the next sabbath. He was called, soon after, to a city church. The church at Fossilville has never been able to settle another pastor, and is still divided on the momentous question of sandwiches. Ham and beef have their respective advocates up to this day.

My friends, I am not to blame for the lightness of my

treatment. I laugh at what I cannot reason down; but underneath my laughter, and almost marring it, I will confess there comes a moan for opportunities lost, for energies mis-spent, for golden chance abused. You know as well as I, that, all up and down New England, churches have been and are being rent by questions of no earthly moment. The church at Fossilville is typical, and Deacon Slowups are everywhere. Stupidity sits in official stations; and bigotry sows dragons' teeth where flowers of Christian fellowship should spring and bloom. In half our churches no new measure, however good, can be proposed, and not meet with persistent opposition. The instant that some plan, inspired of God in zealous hearts, is born, a dozen bony hands clutch at its throat, and strangle it. Progress, instead of being peaceful, is made through such tumult and conflict, that it is almost robbed of profit; and when the needed change at last is made, and one counts up the loss and gain, they so nearly balance that you hesitate to which side to give your verdict. The motto in these churches is, " What has not been shall not be." I could name church after church, where a dozen men sit like leeches on the swelling veins of holy enterprise.

They form a minority powerful in their ignorance and narrowness and stupidity. Their very pigheadedness constitutes their ability to resist what is good. They make it a matter of conscience, and you must batter them over before you can budge them an inch. By them, religion is so advertised that it becomes a target for wit to practise at, and a stumbling-block to the humane. Christ is made to appear hostile to whatever is most honorable in conduct and noble in aspiration. And Christianity, the sweet, the beautiful Christianity of the New Testament, as they interpret it stands like a huge barricade stretched across the path of an onmoving humanity; a thing to be stormed over, and trampled under foot. And so it comes about, that men who need salvation more than life, alienated from our churches by the bigotry and illiberality in them, die unsaved.

I know there is a strong drift all over the land, in our generation, to wash men out into a sea of loose opinions and looser practices. Many are unwilling to abide by the old anchorages, albeit the sea is white outside, and the air filled with patches of froth; and those who are foolish enough to sever the stout cables that held the fathers, and push out into wild and chartless seas, for the most part make wreck, and go down. I tell you, friends, at a time like this, when the intellect of the world is stimulated into an almost frenzied activity; when letters and science are full of contradictions; when a thousand conflicting influences, like the atmospheric commotions of a whirlwind, revolve around us with bewildering violence, and threaten to lift us off our feet, and spin us into the air, — a man must lay hold of certain deeply-rooted, immovable truths, and link his fingers around them. In religion, in politics, in his views of social development, he must have some faith, some deeply-rooted and oaklike confidence, to tie up to. Swinging with a lateral range I care not how far, held by a cable I care not how long, he must, nevertheless, strike his grapnel into the cleft of some immovable rock. I doubt if any who know me would call me a "conservative," as that word now is unfortunately applied; and yet I have not, and never have had, any sympathy with a radicalism which smites gods and mummies alike; that blind, reckless, conceited egotism which refuses to discriminate betweeen the good and the evil, the needed and the useless, of the past; too vain to tread a path ever trodden before, albeit by feet that passed along it to heaven.

The progress I urge, and argue for, is of a different sort. I urge that our churches of all denominations no longer abide by maxims, which, although once proper, are now ill suited to the age. What I wish is to set the strong, lusty present face to face with the weak and wrinkled past; and let the stout lungs of the one breathe a new vitality into the withered bosom of the other. I never let age, alone, sanctify any thing, nor prejudice my mind against it. If a whole catacomb of mummies stood in the path of a Pacific Railroad, I would say to the engineers, "Away with these dry and dusty threads of withered mortality, albeit souls once tabernacled within the circle of these linen investments!" Yet some there are who would call this sacrilege, and gaze in holy reverence at the senseless objects, and sniff with pious delight the scent of ancient embalmment.

My friends, piety does not put a man into a straitjacket. It does not cramp and pucker him up. It does not prescribe the fashion of his necktie, or goose-poke him with spinal stiffness. Those who think that it is an unpardonable sin to row a boat, or shoot a rifle, and ride a horse so as not to make a fool of yourself or kill the horse, are not up in their exegesis.

"THE SYMBOL OF CHRISTIANITY WAS A RENT BANNER," ETC.
Page 37.

These croakers should know that Christianity is not owl-like or bat-like. She does not mope in dismal places; and the most timid child is not afraid to look into her eyes. She is full of adaptiveness. She is many-sided, and swift of foot; and the world, in its fast-racing progressiveness, cannot outrun her. In ages of persecution she showed men her heroic side; and, thus inspired, they went unflinchingly to the stake. In days of revolution, when the world is about to give birth to a higher liberty, she whets the edge of the sword, and swells up in patriotic songs around blazing camp-fires. There have been times in the history of the race, when the symbol of Christianity was a rent banner, her herald a cavalry trumpet, and her pulpit the field men died on. Ours is an age of trade, of commercial combinations, of material development, and scientific investigation. She adapts herself to it; and her symbol to-day is the white sail of a ship, a chemical laboratory, and an axe sunk into the root of a tree.

Is it not strange that some in our churches will not open their eyes enough to see that the world is changing rapidly, and that the Church herself must change in the phases of her experience, and the means and methods of her growth and power? One thing may as well be taken as settled: that, if the Church would direct the age, she must keep in the van of the age. The world is forging ahead, and Deacon Slowups must get out of the way. The Church has been represented by dyspeptic and consumptive men long enough. We have been trying for seventy years, in New England, to run our pulpits on nervous forces alone. It is a failure. The pulpits have broken down under the experience. I hope to live to see the day in Boston City, when a stoop in the back will be unorthodox, and a narrow chest put a theological student at an immense disadvantage in candidating. A church should examine a pastor-elect touching hygiene as closely as touching his theological tenets, and Dio Lewis be recognized as a wise teacher as well as St. Paul. A diseased eye unfits a surgeon for practice, and a diseased stomach unfits a man to use that knife which pierceth to the joints and marrow. All down through history, God has always selected healthy, outdoor men to be his mediums through whom to communicate with the race. Take Moses,— this is not fancy: run over the list,— Joshua, Elijah, David, the apostles, Christ himself: all were out-door men. Adam lived principally in the country; and John saw heaven in vision when camping out on the Isle of Patmos. This thing will settle itself in a few years. Americans are not fools; and they will see which class of men do the most work, and the most telling work.

Bronchitis and consumption — I say nothing against them, though I wish nothing to do with them myself — will be looked upon as a misfortune, and not to be regarded as proof of high scholarship, and soundness in doctrine, as they have been, and are still in many of our rural churches. Why, friends! I know what I am saying. A man who says nothing but what stares at him from a manuscript is not careless of speech. I was born and brought up among people like those I am describing. I have served in country churches for years; I have preached in a parish where the blast of a steam-whistle had never sounded; where to skate was unministerial, and to slide down hill a sin; where the crack of my rifle caused as much excitement in the church as the last trump; and where, if I took a step over fourteen inches and a half from heel to toe, it made the sewing-society lively for two weeks. I think the man who came after me, the present incumbent, could step fourteen feet at a stride, and no one notice that it was longer than common. And yet, to show you how rapidly changes are going

"IT MADE THE SEWING-SOCIETY LIVELY FOR TWO WEEKS."

on in New England, I had not been gone six months before the church came together, and chose two new deacons out of my rifle-club, and they were my best shots at that.

I tell you, friends, the large-hearted, level-headed men in our churches must come to the front. We cannot put pious inefficiency in office much longer. A necklace of six millstones is more than a church can wear, and keep her head above water in as rough seas as heave us around now. Every election in a church should be to a service, and not to a rank; and the man or woman best calculated to do the work, nominated to do it. Then, when by reason of years, or failing health, or change in circumstances, they became unable to do the work intrusted to them, they would naturally resign, or else the church would depose them. I counsel no harshness, no disrespect, no unnecessary wounding of feeling. But when it comes to offending one man, or crippling the usefulness of an entire church, the question is one about which there can be no debate.

There is another typical man whom one can meet in New England,—the harsh, unlovely, wickedly-cunning deacon. Nearly every pastor has met him once at least. I sketch his portrait in profile, and yet I sketch it in charity. I sketch it first as many a pastor sees it sabbath by sabbath, looking from his pulpit, with sad eyes and a sadder heart; and then as every pastor shall see it, let us hope, ere it fades from mortal sight.

Deacon Sharpface was a peculiar man : a very unfortunate man he was, even at birth. His mother was bilious, and his father rheumatic; and he resembled both. To his parental inheritance he had managed to add dyspepsia; and dyspepsia to him meant something. He paid attention to it. He ate with it, and slept with it. It sharpened his countenance, glared ferociously at you through his spectacles, and sounded through his nose when he prayed. He had been a professor forty years, but had been re-converted after he had been a member of the church thirty, and a deacon ten. I find no fault with this. His second conversion was rather needed. Even another would have done him no considerable injury. Spiritually he needed the allopathic treatment, — large doses and frequent administrations.

But, friends, whatever Deacon Sharpface lacked in gentleness, in charity, in the sweet graces of the Spirit, in brotherly kindness, in patience, it mattered little, for he was thoroughly orthodox. That saved him. If he had been a Parkerite, or had worshipped with Brother

DEACON SHARPFACE.

Alger, he would have been a terrible example of what heresy could do. But his orthodoxy saved him. It covered him with a mantle of charity, and won him the election to the deaconate.

That filled his cup to overflowing. It gave him many advantages, chief among which was this: it gave him a lifelong opportunity to defend the old faith. Never did a man improve an opportunity better. Woe to the preacher who preached before Deacon Sharpface, especially if he was a young man! He listened to every sermon, from beginning to end, only to discover heresy. Any unusual form of expression was instantly noted down. If a text was misquoted, he was in ecstasy, and the hard lines of his face absolutely, for once, relaxed as if, somewhere in its cadaverous recesses, there yet remained the corpse of an unburied smile. A sermon was an intellectual refreshment, and prayers he enjoyed pencil in hand. I have said that the deacon was unfortunate, — unfortunate in his nature, his education, and his temper; but his greatest misfortune was the time of his birth. He was born nineteen hundred years too late. He should have been a Pharisee, and a member of the Sanhedrim, at the time of Christ.

Now, you think that is harsh. Well, I will hang the two faces side by side for a moment, and you shall look into their eyes. Like a Pharisee, this New-England deacon was bigoted. It was the joke of the city.

"HE LISTENED TO EVERY SERMON."

Like a Pharisee, he was spiritually proud. Like a Pharisee, he was fond of traditions. What had not the mould and mildew of age upon it must be an error: whatever had, from that fact became the highest wisdom.

Like a Pharisee, he was sharp in his judgments, and bitter in his speech. His wife knew that best. Like a Pharisee, he loved to have his goodness recognized. He loved to have it known in the great gatherings of

"HIS WIFE KNEW THAT BEST."

his denomination, where the lay and clerical dignitaries met, that he was the senior deacon of a great metropolitan organization. But the strength of his position in that church, the granite barricade, behind which the miserable man crouched to cast forth stones at better people than himself, was his undoubted orthodoxy.

My friends, we shall pass, but the influence of our words and deeds will never pass. If wrong be in our lives, then shall it live, and give us evil representation, when we are gone. If good be of us, then, long after we are in our graves, will it grow, and walk the earth in power, and be among the majestic forces of the world. Oh for the discerning eye, therefore; the judgment well instructed, and unbiassed by the pressure of any passion; a conscience quick; and a love which wears the Golden Rule upon its brow, as a queen takes her largest jewel, and binds it to her forehead, on a public day! And here once more I make my record: if orthodoxy means knowledge of words only; if it means defence of ancient forms and usage once valuable, now useless, left, like camps, far in the rear by the world in its progressive movements, which, like an army, stays not in one place, but is forever on the move, inspired by the command to "march on;" if it means a narrow view of men and things; if it arms one hand of God with thunder, but takes the branch of mercy from the other; if it means a clannish love for doctrines based on one of a dozen forms of interpretation, but neglect of charitable practice; if it means bitterness towards any human being, or severance from the growing sense of human brotherhood which now, beyond all other tendencies, represents the pentecostal influence; if it thinks that Boston can be converted by Westminster Catechisms, and not by bread for the starving, clothing for the naked, knowledge for the ignorant, improved dwellings for the poor, and charity toward all, — if it means this, I say, for one, I will have none of it.

If, on the other hand, it uses words as a mirror through which to see the will and wish of God reflected; if it means discarding what was local and temporary in the past, but holding stoutly on to the universal; if it means keeping the old anchors on deck for emergencies of tempest, but spreading below and aloft every inch of canvas for swift traffic in those humanities calculated to elevate the race; if it means the highest culture of the intellect, the widest play of the affections, reverence towards God, and sincere love for all mankind, — if it means this, I say, then will I love it; and it shall be the platform of my utterances in life, and the couch on which, when life is spent, I will lie down in gravity and peace to die.

And so, at last, it seemed to Deacon Sharpface. The years grew on apace; time bore heavily on him; and the forces of his mind and body, like a receding tide, ebbed away. Upon his bed, new visions came to him. At dead of night, in the stillness of his chamber, from which he felt that he should never more go forth until the angels lifted him, angels came, and ministered to his soul. Within his bosom, like a well in a desert, was opened a fountain of new, of precious, and at first of unutterable thoughts. His temper, like a sea long ruffled, whose action was too often like the rush of waves, no longer poured upon by gust and gale of human infirmity, subsided; and its hasty impulses settled gradually but surely to a blessed calm. Its fret and fever left him. His prejudices died out. The haughty pride that had distinguished him left its throne; and sweet Humility timidly, as to an unaccustomed place, came in, and, true to her nature, seated herself upon the footstool. Love stole to her side; and the two, like long-parted sisters, with brimming eyes, and hands joined, — what power might ever part them? — sat there together, saying each to the other, " My sister forever and forever."

The time wore on; and his life, like a rich autumn

day, grew lovelier as it drew to its close. He sent for all his friends. They saw the blessed change, and spoke of it in whispers, marvelling. He sent for all his enemies, — and he had many, — and parted with every man in peace. Last of all he sent a few lines, pencilled with feeble hand, praying that his pastor would come; and he came, the man of God, and stood beside him, all others being decorously without. The deacon took him by the hand, and a smile lit up his features, and sweetened all his face; and he said, —

"My pastor, I have sent for you to tell you what the Lord has done to me in sickness, and rejoice your soul. My eyes are open, brother, and I see as never before. God does not seem as he once did to me: he is not such as I supposed; he is more gracious, more loving. The Bible does not seem as it once did: it is a sweeter book; a revelation, not of wrath and judgment, but of a sweet, a deathless mercy. O my brother! for years I read it wrongly. Men lost by my mistake: but I lost more than they; for I missed peace, and the multiplying joys that come of merciful thoughts, and the rich pleasure of loving. But I see better now; yes, I see better now."

He paused a moment, pressed with weakness. His pastor lifted him upon the pillow, and placed the pillow, with the whiter head upon it, against his own breast. The deacon rested thus a moment, like a tired child, and then he said, —

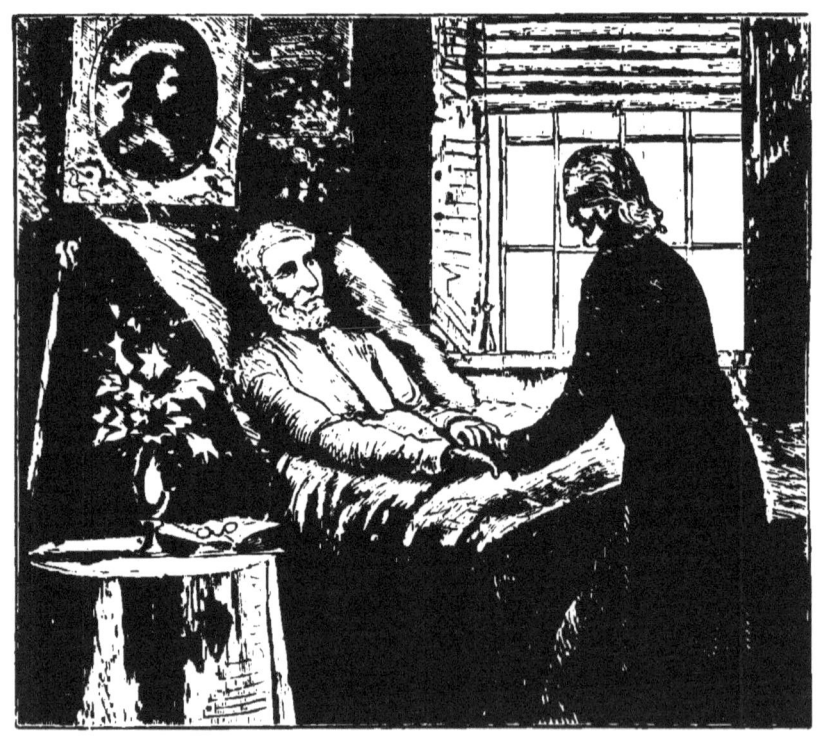

"MY EYES ARE OPEN, BROTHER."

"My pastor, I have wronged you more than once. I might have helped you more, and grieved you less. And here I make the restitution of a dying man: I crave forgiveness. You need not speak: I know I have it, for I know your nature. You thought of God one way, I another; and our natures grew in harmony with our respective thoughts: but now we think alike, and I know your feelings by my own. And now, my brother, the God of whom you told me in the sanctuary, in whom I did not then believe, but do to-day, — the God of infinite mercy bless you! Go on as you have gone: tell men of his love; tell them of his truth; publish his wrath at intervals, only to check the vicious, and make a dark background on which to sketch the whiteness of his mercy. Here on my dying bed, and with my dying breath, remembering all our past differences, and my bitter words, and taking them all back like ashes to my mouth, I simply charge you to go on."

But here the deacon paused. His breath came short and quick, each breath a gasp. He reached his hands up feebly, and drew his pastor's face down to his own, and kissed it, — kissed it twice, once on either cheek; for the two men had drawn so nigh to the kingdom of heaven, that they had become like little children, and, white-headed as they were, were not ashamed to kiss each the other. And then a light broke over all his countenance; a look of wonder and recognition came to his eyes, now dim with that gray mist which comes at last to all of us; his lips parted to speak the words that came not forth, — parted, quivered, closed; and the deacon, prepared at last in understanding to meet his God, prepared in heart to say farewell to men, passed up, to dwell unvexed forever amid the glory of the everlasting light.

My friends, as a public man, I presume I have had my share of enemies. I have probably been pelted up to the full average; at least, I hope the average is not much higher; and this, as one whose path has not been altogether smooth, I wish to say to you: that the longer I live, and the more I know, the larger seems to me the proportion of good men. Never before did the world seem so lovely, or men so kind. Never before did the suffrage in favor of frankness and honesty appear to me so large. The world grows to be more and more delightful in its friendships, and noble in its loves. In the class whose exceptional cases furnish me with my theme, true piety has been the rule, harshness and meanness the exception. Where I have found one to resist, I have found a dozen to applaud. Among these I have found many of my warmest friends; men of the widest knowledge, the most Christlike spirit, and the most progressive minds; men zealous in every good word and work; and now one of these, as my last portrait, I will present. I lift the curtain, and, behold, Deacon Goodheart stands before you.

Deacon Goodheart — may his tribe increase! — was deacon in one of the stiffest Orthodox churches. Of its orthodoxy, according to the letter of the law, there was no doubt. Its creed would have made Calvin himself laugh. There is but one word that precisely describes it: it is "*stiff*." The church was organized in troublesome times. Every now and then, you know, society is seized with a spasm: a wild desire for something new, a desire to tear down and demolish, takes possession of the public mind. It breaks out and rages in the midst of a community, like an epidemic among children, which never kills anybody, but makes the old folks anxious. Well, some sixty years back, Boston had such an experience theologically. It was a pretty sharp attack; and the joints were all loosened, the nerves excited, and every thing shook. The fathers and mothers in Israel, and all those who loved the old order of things, — the word of God as it had been interpreted, and that stern, but magnificent system of ethics, which may make its disciples bigoted, but, at the same time, makes it possible for men and women to sleep safely at night with the doors and windows of their houses unfastened, — these, I say, were alarmed; and certain grouped themselves together, and formed a church. Under such circumstances, it is not surprising, that, when they came to form a creed, they should make it decidedly stiff. They loved the old faith, the faith of the fathers, the faith that had made New England the birthplace of heroic men, and filled their days with toil, and sent them to their graves magnificently, as warriors who sleep at evening on the field they have gloriously won. These, I say, were not ashamed of their faith, and they were willing the city should know it. Whatever was decided, therefore, whatever was unequivocal, whatever was obnoxious to the current opinion, whatever was gnarled and tough and unhewed, in the old faith, they spiked it all in. Their ship was ungainly: its lines were not symmetrical, its masts were short, its sailing-qualities poor.

But you could not sink it; for its compartments were filled with the buoyancy of the gospel, and its sides plated with six-inch proof-texts, and turreted with the thunders of the law. More than once have the wit and culture of the city laughed at its ungainliness, and the sceptic darkened the air around it with the arrows of his sarcasm: but more than once have wit and culture acknowledged with pride its steadfastness; and more than once has New England rocked when its turrets began to revolve for action.

Of such a church, severe, strict, with a hypocrite and bigot here and there in it, our friend was elected deacon. His election was a miracle; that is, unaccountable. In physique he was not exactly corpulent, I won't say that: but he was, to put it mildly, a little stout; and who ever knew of an old-type orthodox church having a fat man for a deacon? He was an anomaly, and as large a one as could be gotten in and out of a pew-door. I cannot say how tall he was. I never thought of his height: no one ever did when he saw him. It was not his height, but his thickness, you thought of. The deacon, to say the least, was voluminous, ample, and generous. His countenance was full and florid, — a fact which should have cost him twenty votes at his election; and, when he laughed, it shook and wrinkled and flushed until it looked no more like a deacon's than a forty-pound watermelon looks like a little warty, shrivelled, crooked-necked gourd. The deacon served as usher at the Rectangular Church. That word slipped off my pen before I knew what was coming; formed itself, as it were, out of the ink. But why I should call it the Rectangular Church, I can hardly say; perhaps because the name, by the law of association of ideas, suggested itself naturally from the strictness of its doctrines; perhaps because, like authors who cudgel their brains for a name for a book, or clergymen who write a logical sermon before they select a text, and then take whatever they hit upon, — you see, I know how it is done, — no matter how this is, the deacon served as usher at the Rectangular Church. And what an usher he was! To see him come sailing down the aisle, his face beaming a benignant welcome upon you; to be addressed as if the whole church belonged to you, and you have only to elect your favorite sitting, when every seat is jammed; to have him act as if your coming was a personal favor, and the service would not have been quite complete without your presence, — surely such an usher is invaluable. Why, friends, Deacon Goodheart's face, hung over the front entrance of a church that didn't cost over one hundred thousand dollars, could fill every seat in it within ten minutes. I limit the cost; for, when a church-edifice costs over a certain sum, it is not built for the people to worship in, and the masses know it; and there are churches, and in Boston too, that neither the faces of forty Deacon Goodhearts, nor the faces of forty angels either, could ever persuade the common people, the like of whom heard the Saviour gladly in their time, to enter. Deeper than reason, friends, deeper than education, there is in the human heart an instinct which warns the modest, the poor, and the proud where not to go. These cathedrals of exclusiveness, these palaces of wealthy piety, into which no angels enter, save such as money has painted on the tinted glass, and etched upon the smooth ceilings; these temples of æsthetic piety, built by the few, for the few, — are useless for the great, onpushing work of redeeming man. Away with these vast piles of chiselled stone, these ornamental sepulchres of free utterance, these mausoleums where sleeps the spirit of that warm brotherhood which had a common treasure! and give us buildings large enough for all, and free to all.

Then shall great preachers arise, men as great in utter-

"THESE CATHEDRALS OF EXCLUSIVENESS."

ance as the truths they are sent to proclaim, equally inspired of God; and the gospel be no longer peddled from house to house, but preached with an eloquence as classic as the Greeks, and as fervid as Isaiah's lofty

verse; churches that shall seat thousands of all faiths
and creeds, drawn to one assemblage not by the egotism
of common belief, which small men deem the basis of
fellowship, but by the craving of a quick intelligence
thirsting for knowledge, by the attraction which the
larger and magnetic has for the smaller and less inspired,
and by the certainty that the independence of the
intellect shall be acknowledged, and none abused for
what they might not help, the errors of their thinking.
But that day will never dawn upon this city; or, if
it comes, a change will first come to the hearts of the
men who dictate taste and fitness to us. This Commonwealth must first feel the shame of its heathenism, the
shame of its low-browed ignorance, the shame of its
red-eyed drunkenness, the shame of its popular brothels, its swarming jails, and the perils of its brute-necked violence, or ever churches will be built to serve
the end which alone justifies their erection.

But Deacon Goodheart was something more than an
usher: he was the best of deacons. He was not rich in
money, and yet no one deemed him poor; for the church
all felt that he had great riches laid up somewhere ahead
of him, and that he would come to them one day, and

be as rich as the richest. His pastor loved him best, because he knew him best; for he knew him in his deeds; and who knows a Christian until he knows him so? He heard his name spoken in love by the poor and sick, and those whom the great roaring world forgets because of their littleness; and more than once, when kneeling himself beside a humble bed in some narrow room, he had heard the deacon's name spoken with gratitude, and coupled with blessing, with that greatest name given under heaven and among men; spoken by lips that smiled in dying, but which would have had no smile had it not been for what the deacon's teaching and alms had done for them. His praise was spoken in lowly places, — in chambers of neat poverty, in the hushed room of sickness, and in those little narrow dormitories built for the indigent aged. In places such as these, and not in public halls and on the great exchange, his praise was mentioned: where else? In heaven: is yours, friend?

The deacon had his faults; but they seemed, like the stains upon a lady's garment, the result of accident, not of design. They were of nature, and not of will; a kind of birthmark inherited from Adam, or some one way back. His face was like a full moon, flushed with summer's warmth: you remember how it looks, — a perfect sphere of beaming benignity. Mirth looked laughingly out of his eyes, peered roguishly from the corners of his mouth, and sat demurely on his rounded chin. His face was a constant challenge to humor. The language of its look was, "Say something funny, and see me laugh." The children all loved him, of course. He won their love by loving them. I doubt if any of us had loved God, did we not know that he first loved us. Whenever he came in sight, they swarmed around him. They would climb his knees and back, and perch upon his shoulders, and cling laughingly around his neck, until he looked like a pyramid covered with morning-glories. He had no children after the flesh himself; but he counted his children after the spirit by scores and hundreds, and was a kind of universal father to them all. And, when the deacon dies, his going hence will make more children glad in heaven, and sad on earth, than the death of any other man I know.

Ecclesiastically, judged by the traditional standard, the deacon was entirely unsuited to his office. He was not great in prayer; that is, he did not tell the Lord all that he had done, and how he came to do it, since the creation; which was not deacon-like. I never heard him begin with Genesis but once; and then he got no farther than the Food, when he lost his footing, and broke down. Worse even than this peculiarity, was the fact that his memory was so bad, that he never used the same prayer twice; which is an unpardonable eccentricity in a deacon. Indeed, he was full of imperfections. He would often make an exhortation without quoting a text of scripture. He very rarely wept when he spoke, which detracted materially from his influence with a certain class; nor did he ever boast what the Rectangular Church had done in the past, and congratulate mankind in general that it still existed. In fact, he was a very queer and most extraordinary deacon. His prayers were simple, direct, and confidential as a child's first penitential talk with a gentle-hearted, sweet-faced mother; although at times his voice would swell into a tone of exultation, and a light spread over his lifted face, as if, in answer to his prayer, some angel had come down, and was hovering for a moment, on wings of light, above his raised countenance. Nor was he fluent. At times he stammered; but his stammering sounded like the hesitation of a lowly person called upon to plead his cause before a king, and who scarcely knew how to express himself in such a presence. And once he broke entirely down, came to a dead stop. He was praying, that evening, for those who did not pray for themselves,— for those " unblessed ones," as he expressed it, " who do not know the joy of holy utterance, or how sweet a thing it is to talk with thee, O God!" And here the thought of their deprivations oppressed him, or else he missed the proper word; for he staggered in speech, and suddenly sat down; and a great silence fell on the room, and no one, of all the hundreds present, lifted his head for a full minute; and nothing was heard unless it was a smothered sob here and there. But, in spite of this verbal deficiency, the people loved to hear him; and the business men who knew him on the street, and who made money many times faster than he, listened respectfully to him when he spoke to them in meeting, touching the manner of life which they should live day by day in order to gain the better life to come.

But it was what he did, and his way of doing it, and

not what he said, that made his name so fit and mirror-like to his character.

It was night — a night such as the rich love, and the poor hate; cold, bitter, and piercing. The air was full of snow, soggy and damp; while ever and anon a shower of sleet half-frozen, mingled with hail, plunged downward, or was slashed heavily against the walls of the houses. The winds were rampant: they roared around the corners, careered along the streets, shook the shutters of the houses, and wrestled at the lamp-posts until the gas-jets flared and sputtered in deadly fear lest they should be extinguished. It was a night to be remembered in mansion and garret alike. How warm the velvet carpet, how cheerful the glowing grate, how rich the dark woods look, how gay the laughter sounds, and how the swell of music rises, where love and plenty sit when the storm roars without, and the snow drives against the curtained pane! What a sense of comfort, and the luxury of warmth, steals over one as he sits, slippered and gowned, before the red coals on such a night! Never is warmth so warm, never luxury so luxurious, never wealth so satisfactory, as then.

"IT WAS NIGHT."

But to those who live in garrets, or burrow in cellars, such a night is terrible. Black as the heavens seems to them their fate. Oh the lack of clothing! oh the absence of light! How the old rookery shakes as the gale smites it! How the snow sifts through the ill-thatched roof, or whirls in eddies across the uneven floor! How the healthy curse, and the sick moan, and the drunken rave or lie in leaden sleep, while the limbs stiffen, and the soul steals shiveringly out of the unwarmed body, and is borne away by the colder winds!

It was on such a night that Deacon Goodheart left his snug home, his warm fireside, and his loving spouse, who muttered at his going, and yet, womanlike, loved him all the better in her heart for doing it, and started out in search of those who needed the Christian's loaf and the Christian's presence. Few deacons, I ween, were on the streets that night. It is so much easier, you know, good friends, to pray for the poor in your snug chambers, with your hands laid softly on the warm flannel and the white pillow waiting you, than to go forth into the cold snow, and wade your way toward the fulfilment of your prayer. But the good deacon — God bless him, and all like him, in and out of the church! — had a queer theology; and he held that He who works by means, and not by miracles, makes man the agent by whom to answer his own prayers; and he used to say, — but the senior deacon of the church called it rank heresy, — he used to say that deacons never prayed aright unless they went and did themselves what they asked God to do. Thus upheld, buttoned to the chin, and warmly gloved, he opened the door of his dwelling, and plunged out into the darkness.

Now, the deacon was no gymnast. He had never practised on the trapeze. He was large, as I have hinted, and not remarkably agile. The snow lay a foot in depth, the flagging was iced beneath; and, as he stepped boldly off into the drift, some of you may imagine the result. The deacon slipped, — even deacons do make a slip occasionally, — the deacon slipped, I say; slipped with both feet at once; slipped, and sat down. It was well done, as only a deacon of his size could do it. He was a man of decision, and he sat down decidedly. His first thought was of his wife. Had she seen him? Horrors! if she had! He knew that he closed the

"HE TWISTED HIMSELF ABOUT," ETC. Page 73.

door behind him; but had she, in her loving anxiety, followed him? and were her affectionate eyes now fastened on him? He twisted himself about, and cast a look of agony at the door. Blessed absence! her darling face was not there. But had she heard him? She *must* have. It seemed to him that he had shaken the entire block when he struck the pavement. But *no:* the good woman had resigned him to the care of Providence when he left her, and Providence was now dealing with him alone. Yes, he was unobserved. A feeling of sweet complacency stole over him. There are positions perfectly honorable in themselves, but in which a man does not like to be looked at. The deacon started to get up: he succeeded only in part. He discovered, with Carlyle, that "our successes are part failures." He lifted himself on his palms to the full length of his arms; and there he hung a moment, hung dubiously, and then sat down again. The deacon laughed. Friends, I never eulogize deacons: no man ever heard me; no one ever will. I had no intention of eulogizing Deacon Goodheart; but I submit that it is not every man that can laugh all to himself, without company, after he has sat down on an icy pavement as decidedly as the good deacon had. I said he began to laugh. That laugh started him. He began to slide. The more he slid, the louder he laughed; and, the more he laughed, the faster he slid. He slid as

"THE MORE HE SLID, THE LOUDER HE LAUGHED."

if he were greased. He slid like lightning. He swept the sidewalks like an orthodox whirlwind. He lost his personality, and looked more like a dozen coal-hods tied together, than an officer of the Rectangular Church, as he came bowling along. At last he finished his declension, and began to feel the reward of the backslider. He was literally "filled with his own ways:" ears, eyes, mouth, shared in the punishment. He shook himself, stamped, smote his sides with his palms until he was tolerably free from snow, and started on. He was now in a section of the city where the poor and dissolute live. He was pushing on, when a low sound arrested his step. He paused to listen, and again he heard it, and this time caught the direction. It came from the second story of an old house on his left.

The deacon clomb the stairs, which creaked and groaned beneath his weight like a living thing in torture: he reached the hall above, and paused to listen. A feeble moan penetrated the dividing wall, stole out into the cold air, and died away amid the roaring of the storm. It was a child's voice, and the sadness of it touched him deeply. He took a traveller's candlestick from out his pocket, felt for a dry spot on the wall to draw the match, and lighted it. A door was right before him. A noble door it had been once, of dark wood choicely wrought — a door through which the youth and beauty of departed generations had often passed in the full pride of their rich loveliness; but now 'twas scarred and dinted as if by blows of a hatchet, or of rough things roughly thrown; and one carved panel had been knocked entirely out. He lifted the latch, and stepped into the room. Would that I had the power to sketch that room as the deacon saw it on that night, that, sitting here in all this light and comfort, you might take down to your warm homes a picture of one room like those in which the children of poverty and sin are born, and live and die! It was the home of desolation. Cheerlessness and discomfort reigned supreme. Their sway was never challenged. The fireplace was unlighted by a spark. A heap of sodden ashes, and a mound of snow, lay on the sunken and cracked hearthstone. One of the two windows was roughly boarded up; and the sash of the other bulged with rags stuffed coarsely in. There were no chairs. A mutilated table stood close against the wall, evidently so placed to steady it; and a rude bench, some six feet long, without a back, and rudely hacked, was drawn up in front of it. In the farther corner stood a bedstead, or what had once been one; but now

A HOME OF DESOLATION. 77

the posts, which once were long, had been sawn off, and the headboard wrenched away, doubtless for fuel. A heap of unbound straw, covered by an old blanket, composed the bed. It was a bed barely fit for a dog to

"IT WAS THE HOME OF DESOLATION."

lie on; and yet a girl lay on it, and a girl, too, born in the mould of beauty. The deacon stood and gazed upon her. In years she might have seen eight winters. The happy reckon life by summers, friends; but wretchedness counts its life by its experiences of suffering; and so I say the girl that lay groaning on that blanket might have seen eight winters. Her face was white as the snow upon the floor, and almost as cold. Her little features were shrunken; hunger had eaten away their fulness; and where your child, mother, has a plump, round cheek, centred with a dimple which you have kissed a thousand times, this wan cheek showed only a depression. And yet, emaciated as it was, the face was lovely. Starvation and sickness had done their utmost, and yet had left it beautiful. Her hair was of the color of yellow gold shaded with bronze, and fine as unwoven silk blown out of nature's loom; and its tangled wealth swathed the coarse pillow, and framed her white face in like a rich aureole such as the old painters, the great masters of color, loved to paint around the heads of their Madonnas. Her eyes were of that gray which darkens in feeling, and looks out at the object of their love through a rich mist, when the soul swells up into the face in moments of passion; and, as she lifted them to the deacon's countenance wonderingly, they seemed, in contrast to her small white face, strangely yet beautifully large and luminous. The deacon sat upon the edge of the bed, and took her thin hands in his, and said, "My little girl, what is your name?" and she, in a low, weak voice, replied, "My name is Mary, sir; and who be you?"—"My name," the deacon answered, "is Goodheart; and I have come to make you warm and well and happy." She looked at him for a moment with her large bright eyes, as if in doubt that he spoke honestly; and then half querulously, as the sick often answer, said, "You have been a long while coming, sir."—"But I am here at last," the deacon returned, cheerfully humoring her conceit; and his great, round face, sweet as a woman's in its goodness, lighted up as he spoke: "I am here at last, Mary; and now I am going right to work to make you comfortable, and get you well."—"I never shall get well, sir," she replied: "I am going to die, and be put in the ground."—"Oh, no, you are not!" returned the deacon. "You must get well. You don't wish to die, do you?"—"Yes, sir, I do," she answered. "I did not wish to once, when I could run about, and keep warm. But it is so cold here, sir! I guess I shall be warmer in the ground;" and a shiver ran through her little frame, and sharpened her tiny features. The deacon rose. A startled look came to his face. Could it be that the child was dying? He pulled off his great fur coat, and placed it over her (it was so large it covered all the bed); and then he knelt beside her, and smoothed back the tangled strands of golden hair that swept her forehead, and soothed her with low murmurs as a mother soothes her babe; and warmth came back to her little half-frozen limbs, and she made a motion as when a child nestles for sleep; and the fringed lids drooped over the waxen skin, as a light shadow outlines itself upon the snow in moonlight.

The deacon smiled. His face brightened in hope; and he said to himself, "If she can only sleep!" and then aloud, "Mary, I must leave you for a little time. I am going to get some wood, and make a nice, warm fire, and bring you medicine and some food; and to-morrow I shall take you home with me; and, if you wish, you shall never leave me, but always stay, and be my little girl." The deacon said this chokingly; for his heart went out strangely toward the little thing, as one, through suffering and neglect, given by God to him. And then, rising, he bent down over her, and whispered, "Do you think that you shall sleep now, Mary?" And she softly, as a child speaks, and makes reply in drowsiness, answered, "Yes, sir: I shall sleep."

An hour passed by, and the deacon entered the room again, loaded with fuel, and supplies of comfort. He filled the fireplace with wood, and kindled it, and stood a moment, as the flames leaped up, and dried his wet hands. And then he lifted the candle from the floor, and stepped softly to the bed. Mary lay still hidden away under the great robe. He smiled, and said, "The child sleeps, and the child shall live!" He placed his hand upon the cover, and folded it slowly and gently back, until her face, pillowed amid its wealth of golden hair, was seen, sad and white and still. The deacon gazed a moment doubtingly. He bent his face down over hers. A moment he held it there; and then he lifted it. A look of reverent awe, a look as of one who has come near to God, came to his countenance; and he said, "The child does indeed sleep, and the child shall indeed live; but her sleep is not the slumber of this earth, and her life is that forever lived with God."

And then, as if stricken with the sense of some great loss, the fading out of some bright hope that had suddenly come to him, and as suddenly left him, the deacon knelt; and bowing his head upon his crossed arms, while the wind roared outside, and the firelight died away in ghostly glimmers along the wall, he broke out, and sobbed aloud.

www.ingramcontent.com/pod-product-compliance
Lightning Source LLC
Chambersburg PA
CBHW020329090426
42735CB00009B/1468